Pennies from Heaven

Poems 2003-2010

L.E. Ward

iUniverse, Inc.
New York   Bloomington

Pennies from Heaven
Poems 2003-2010

iUniverse books may be ordered through booksellers or by contacting:

iUniverse
1663 Liberty Drive
Bloomington, IN 47403
www.iuniverse.com
1-800-Authors (1-800-288-4677)

Because of the dynamic nature of the Internet, any Web addresses or links contained in this book may have changed since publication and may no longer be valid.

ISBN: 978-1-4502-5810-4 (sc)
ISBN: 978-1-4502-5811-1 (ebk)

Printed in the United States of America

iUniverse rev. date: 9/24/2010

In memory of my mother,
Lillian Estelle Mager Ward,
My lifetime best friend
Whose patience was heaven-sent,
Whose loyalty never wavered

And in appreciation of friends
Donald Aucutt
John Henley
Dr. Charles Hanson, Ph. D.
And Stephen G. Durham

Other Books of Classic Poetry
By L. E. Ward, published by I.universe

The Collected Poems of L. E. Ward

Portraits of Life
The Child Who Loved Movies
The Land Within
The Secret Life of L. E. Ward
The Country of the Heart

Contents

PREFACE

A year or so ago, I encountered a mechanical wizard named Zoltan the Magnificent in an antique store, who predicted, You will come into a great fortune. Remember, a fortune need not mean money.

I always loved my writing, which I began at home in seventh grade. I love my six published volumes of poetry, beginning with my Collected Poems in 1999. I wrote my first poem in January 1975.

I am happy herewith to present my seventh book collection, which I have worked on since 2003. I love my writing because it expresses my memories and emotions, as well as my hopes for a more humane world--in spite of the odds, and much past and present .historical evidence to the contrary. Written words and memories help to sustain, inspire, and comfort me. While one always hopes for an audience, my poems are a labor of love and always have been, a labor, both for recognition of a human past and a more humane future. They are, in their way, my posterity, and I hope they will survive me, as my legacy -- not of money or stocks or jewels, but as the wealth of a human treasury. Go little book...

L.E. Ward
June 26, 2010

One Book, My Book

I have always loved
Those films or plays
In which a soldier
Carries with him a book,

As if that were
A reality of peace
And beauty in a common world,
Unknown or denied to men.

I have carried this book,
My book, within me,
Thro ugh all the days
The years of earthly

Heaven and hell alike.
These words, these pages,
My rod and my staff,
That comfort me, that comfort me.

The Lighthouse

The light, its light,
Is small, particularly

In comparison to
Many other things.

Still, it has its place,
Its usefulness,

As hope, haven,
Inspiration, beacon.

And without it,
There'd be only

The night, the waves,
The darkness.

Lament

What is keeping you
From compassion, beloved.
Is it your lamp, your lands,
Your table with ornate legs?

What is keeping you
From mercy,
For the outcast, the poor,
The dog that begs?

Are you content, beloved,
Because you are strong?
If that is all,
Why is there war and death and wrong?

O see we are all passing,
momentary passengers on earth,
And there is the common end,
And the heart alone has human worth,

Though every man
Clings to his own lucre
And dwells each to himself,
Every being to its prison.

Vignettes

A radio sounds on a 1950's afternoon,
Strike two... ball four,
And its echo resounds for decades,
Down poetry's corridors.

In the 1950s, Jack Bailey, a brash radio
m.c., would ask his audiences weekdays,
Would You Like To Be Queen for a Day?--
To which they would answer, Yaaas.

We are all a bit like that,
Royalty, here for a day,
But only for a day,
Our day -- not to stay.

Citizen Kane (1941)

We do not ever really sense the future,
Except in terms of educated guesses, intuition.
Yet how could Orson Welles not have expected
His travesty, an inverse mirror reflection,

Of William Randolph Hearst, not
To upset his Hollywood apple cart?
Of course, it was really as an iconoclast,
A terrible young man, that RKO welcomed him,

Or, rather, at its owner,
Nelson Rockefeller's suggestion.
Talk about biting the hand that fed.
Yet, also, let's not forget

The sheer artistry, as well as
Bravura, showmanship, of the thing.
The various bystanders interviewed
On screen by a reporter, one by one,

Like pieces in a puzzle,
Such as Susan Alexander Kane,
In her loneliness, in her emptiness,
Was infatuated with.

Welles, a child of the New Deal,
Created this monster of acquisition,
The junk, a warehouse, of the ages,
And the sled, Rosebud,

A profane, rather than sacred, allusion
Finally uncovered by cinema detectives
Yet on the screen a fabulous

Treatment of the famous, a fable

Like Kubla Khan, like Ozymandius,
Look on my works and despair.
As in life, it is the canvas
Little moments that illuminate, really:

Bernstein's reminiscence of a girl
With a parasol, briefly glimpsed,
Yet never forgotten.
The truth that death comes to all men.

The world a fallen paradise,
A makeshift, counterfeit Eden,
Where everything, great and small,
Human and inhuman, fails in the end.

Sunset Blvd. (1950)

We now know the place,
Thanks to Hollywood and Billy Wilder,
The decaying mansion
With the crazy lady inside

A relic of the good old days,
Grandiose if not grand.
For how grand is anything that fades
As the days, the years, move inexorably onward?

Norma Desmond's address,
She who said, We had faces then…
I'm still big, it's the pictures
That got small

.Long finger nailed, turban wearing,
Devotee of a pet chimpanzee,
A castaway of the jungle, too,
Given a midnight burial.

Gloria Swanson played her,
In her own comeback, at over 50,
As if 50 years were some immense expanse,
As it is, but only in terms of adolescence.

The pictures were new then, young then,
screwy as they were and are,
People sitting in the dark,
Idolizing images in front of them,

Just because in size they're large.
Still Norma had hope, a survivor,
Until her fickle escort decided to leave,

As the days and how many fair-weather

Acquaintances leave us all in the lurch?
Norma had self-love, but Max the butler
Unselfish love, himself a director and
Former husband, reduced to servant,

Swanson's own comeback in the part
Was nominated, giddy but minor.
She told Judy Holliday, It was my only chance
For an Oscar, you had next year.

So do we all, vain ghosts that we are,
If only until the show of life closes.

The Parade of Life

The men, women, and children
Line the small town streets,
Circa the Great War,

Which in time to come
Will become merely World War One,
A power struggle,

As each and every war,
And every life and Life itself,
Will always be, as it always has been.

The women in long dresses, wearing flowered hats;
None aware of the great lost Past,
Lost for all of its smallness and greatness.

The men in suits and hats, amid children,
The soldiers marching past, in lock-step;
All headed for oblivion.

No need to hasten death or praise it,
Although what else is the point of such foolishness,
All unaware of their place in a much-longer procession.

All About Eve (1950)

Eve, Eve, who else but Eve,
Dear Eve, as Margo called her
In her envy as Addison called her,
In his sarcasm.

Blame it on a woman,
The woman, as many,
If not all, of the ancients did.
Blame Eve, commoner, conniver,

Pretender to the throne.
But Mankiewicz,
As director-scenarist, also
Exposed the rest of them,

People of the theatre,
Above it all, above the movies,
For instance, but not above
Pettiness, conceit, narcissism.

Give the Yahoos, the unwashed masses
Of the hinterlands,
Everywhere outside Manhattan,
A treat -- a look-see at the

Feet of clay of the favored few,
The chosen few, yet
Retain a soup con of glamour,
Amid the in-fighting and tribulation.

As Bette Davis once said,
The best acting
in Hollywood never took

place before the cameras.

Hollywood, the offshoot,
The despised, popular cousin.
I am a critic of the theatre.
In it, I toil not, neither do I spin,

George Sanders as the
Adder Addison, the wit De Witt, said.
And all those of us not famous,
As usual, sat glued to our seats,

Addicted to every word,
Hungry as any stage door
Jenny or Johnny for the
False step, the next revelation.

Degas: The Absinthe Drinker

She sits alone, young, drab, melancholy,
At a table, with her drink.
Like her, we exist while we're able,
And our life is our life,

Although death, not life,
Is our ultimate destination.
What sadness, what disappointment,
Led her to this, is the question.

Art, not breath, is the longer span,
For in the paint, alone,
A kind of saint, minor goddess,
She endures, however modest.

The Magnificent Ambersons (1942)

The genteel Midwest, rendered
On RKO sets,
We ramble the days,
As they rambled their rooms,

The last grand ball
At the mansion,
Before the automobile came,
Driving luxury into the outskirts,

The suburbs,
Before industry made the towns
Themselves resemble a quagmire,
A hell on earth.

Georgie, the spoiled son;
Fanny, the nervous spinster-aunt;
The Major, perplexed by his own death.
For some to prevail, others succumb.

Yet all succumb to Time.
Fanny by her stove,
Not caring if it burned her,
Poverty already had.

We ramble the days,
We ramble the years,
But Doom awaits,
Like it awaited even the mansion.

Hollywood Heaven

Say again their names, of movie fortune and fame,
People we usually never met,
Yet with whom we were intimately acquainted,
Down to their every feature, tic, intonation.

Say again their names,
Images, shadows, we met in the dark,
As illuminations of the human condition.
Say again their names,

For all the entertainment, escape, and joy
They gave us, time and time again,
Images larger-than-life, who rose above us,
And yet who became a part of us --

Of our inner, human lives, that is --
Scarlett and Rhett, Rick and Ilsa, Dorothy and Toto,
Charles Foster Kane, Norma Desmond,
Mortal beings captured in an immortal medium.

In Memory of Janet Leigh

The magic worked when it did.
We know history by results.
Not might-have-beens.

At any rate, Norma Shearer,
By then, 1946, a retired queen
Of MGM, spotted her photograph,

A photograph of Jeanette Morrison,
As she was known then,
At a ski-resort; introduced her.

The studio screen-tested,
And the rest is a semi-legend.
It's interesting, she confided,

On later years, to see oneself,
On film, as one looked once upon
A time, in earlier years.

In those days, movies came and went.
There were no residuals. If you
Missed them, we thought, that was it.

Film, unlike life, can endure,
If preserved, as only art does.
As in the celluloid rain,

As a petty thief, Marion Crane,
She drives to the Bates Motel,
To be butchered time after time again.

Pennies from Heaven

When I was a child, growing up in the 1950's,
My parents would recall the 1930's,
The Great Depression,
When jobs were scarce, times were hard.

My father was a painter and decorator;
My mother a legal and real estate secretary.
They married in 1936, and bought our house in 1939,
Instead, as my mother used to say,

Of just paying rent…
And having nothing to show for it.
On other, later occasions, she would sometimes say,
I like my home, to see the few things

I was able too accumulate in my lifetime.
The fascists try to control things,
Life, history, eternity, even,
But the human cling to the human things..

Ghosts

I remember sitting on my neighbor's
Front porch in the early 1950's,
Playing Monopoly with my neighbor friends,
Brothers, both somewhat younger than myself,

With that elderly, white-haired, and
Mustached gentleman, who, like God,
Pronounced his judgments:
Go to Jail, Do Not Pass Go.

The older brother usually won.
His younger brother, sometimes noticing
Two nuns in their habits, walk by,
Would announce, Ghosts!

They moved with their family to Texas in 1958,
And I never saw any of them again.
All our days, our years, are like that, in the end,
Gone up like wisps of air; puffs of smoke.

The Asphalt Jungle (1950)

No less primitive
Than the original,
Merely developed in
Technology, creature comforts,

First glimpsed by me as a child
In previews of coming attractions:
The killer who only killed on
Rainy nights

In "Follow Me Quietly" (1949);
Thugs wearing hoods, sheets,'
In "Storm Warning" (1951),
Common in greed, violence,

Mirrors of the jungle of
Origin, journey, and destination,
Of nightmares and night streets,
Which offered only the inhuman.

A world aswim with shadows,
Not merely because of limited budgets,
But atmosphere, perception,
And a cacophony of self-pity:

I never loved anyone, Walter;
He used to be a big shot;
Top of the world, Ma. Top of the world!
I did my best for you, Veda.

Corrine Calvet in "Rope of Sand" (1949):
I learned early it's the way
Of the world, and not to fight it.
Although struggle everyone does, and did.

Regardless of the impossible odds,
Stacked deck, foregone conclusion,
The members of the rat race only rats, race.
In the way that no one wins. Everyone loses.

Gods

Since time began,
Men have created gods in their own images,
In the interests of
An inclusive immortality.

By contrast, those I knew
And loved in life, on earth,
Were mortal, merely mortal.
But I loved them, nevertheless.

The Old Days

I miss them,
The hustle, bustle,
Of ordinary days,

Real, but doomed,
Mother shopping,
Going to town,

Making meals.
Dad coming home,
Noon-times, for lunch.

Mother saying,
In the afternoon,
She saw and talked

With so-and-so,
About such-and-such,
Uptown.

Gone except from
Memory, gone one day
Except if one is lucky,

Still present in poems,
Home and life and love.
Oh. How I loved them.

Lot's Wife

Of course, I looked back.
It was impossible not to,
At the sight and sounds of
Pets, lovers, people, houses,
Perishing, all perishing.

Of course, I looked back.
It is all and only and always
A holocaust, of course, even if
You don't hear the screams,
See the flames...

It is all and only and always
A holocaust, all our years,
The years, reduced to ash,
To cinders, except in the
Human heart, which remembers.

The Great Fire of London, 1666

First the plague,
And now this:
The bodies
Piled high in carts,

All the while,
The still lucky,
The still living,
Sing hymns, attend the theatre.

The bodies burned
In a bonfire.
Life itself is a bonfire,
All history is a bonfire, the bonfire.

What can we turn to then?
But the breath while
It still exists --
The sacred hearth, the human heart?

Autumn Song

Alas, poor Yorick,
I knew him well,
Shakespeare said that Hamlet said,
While holding Yorick's skull.

So it is on earth,
As it has always been, and will always be.
The skull holds mystery --
The only mystery.

Housewifery

I remember that on certain Sunday afternoons,
In the 1950's and 1960's, my mother
Would come into our living room and say,
How about a pie, apple or blueberry?
She delighted in being kind, in homemaking.
In the 1950's she was equally in charge
Of the local Cancer Society loan-closet.
Not for credit, but if I can help somebody.

We were Methodists, but Sunday evenings,
Attended a gospel missionary church,
Whose women's circle met
Once a month on Tuesday evenings.

At one meeting, my mother,
The secretary-treasurer, turned heads
By saying, Even if there were no heaven,
Shouldn't we want to be kind, anyway
.
So, too, the ignored sun, itself,
Rises every day, giving earth,
Our mortal lives, themselves,
Their passing, fleeting opportunity.

In Memory of D.H. Lawrence

In spite of the condemnation of flesh,
Every person you see on the street
Is a result of an act of sex.

In spite of the rules of clerics and clerks,
Whether bare-chested or silk-shirts,
All run out of time, within Time, and nothing works.

Once all the world was ocean ---
The part that became land overflowed.
Humanity is the only human matter which matters.

Delacroix: Jacob Wrestling with the Angel

In the paint, the two vital, virile, young men
Tussle, wrestle, by a path, a woods, a glen.
The only really striking thing,
Is that one of them has wings.
So, too, each being struggles with life,
Its life, all its life, if not more,
Only to be returned, primal, in the end,
Primal, to the jungle's primal floor.

Willinck; Simon the Stylite

What has killed throughout history like idealism,
Whether in the name of race, nation, or religion.

In the paint, the small, bald man, swathed
In white cloth,
Sits alone, aloof, aloft, atop

A white pillar, all his days, all the days,
His back to the burning, human city behind
Him -- all ablaze.

Edward Hopper's Early Sunday Morning

The several main street shops,
Some with blinds, awnings,
Stand vacant, idle, in the morning.

What has inspired the handshake,
Pleasant Good Morning,
Like the prospect of lucre, money?

Still, without a human presence,
Its certain something,
Life is paltry, empty, without meaning.

Edward Hopper; Gas, A Painting, 1940

Nothing lasts. All things must pass.
Easily enough said. Harder to experience.
In the paint, the manager still attends
His small, roadside station's three tanks.

Like a good and faithful servant,
And will, at least as long as the painting lasts.
How I loved those days, those years,
When all the people I loved and knew were alive,

Were still alive, and would be for
Years, the many years, ahead --
The earth our vehicle, the sun its engine --
In the years in which life, itself, was
Our only daily destination.

Portraits of 19th Century Young Men

William Glackens: Portrait of Charles Fitzgerald

Tall, dark, and handsome,
Well-dressed, a patron of art,
His eyes almost hurt-looking,
His mouth almost a red scar,

His time on earth finished,
In the paint, alone, he now exists,
Persists, as in life,
As if in a realm apart.

James McNeill Whistler: Portrait of
Arthur Jerome Eddy

The painter's lawyer and patron,
A gentleman down to his gloves,
He persists, continues to exist,
In the paint he, also, loved.

Most men worship the patriarchs,
But I, also, have this great mother
In my heart, as he abides as a
Prince in the kingdom of Art.

The Ballad of Lost Players

Where are they now,
The people we used to know,
In shows to which we'd go.
They've vanished like last year's snow.

Where are they now, the faces of yesteryear,
Louis Calhern, Sydney Greenstreet, Anne Revere,
Who gave us cheer and fear and tears?
They've disappeared in Time's maelstrom severe.

Where are they now,
Those we met as shadows amid the shadows?
On earth, they are no more.
Time bestows but it, also, winnows.

Where are they now, the many memorable characters,
Claude Rains, Eve Arden, Thelma Ritter?
On film, they still endure, persevere,
And, if film is preserved, on Film, they will
Live forever.

Peyton Place (1957)

Every town has scandals,
Skeletons in the cemetery,
As well as in closets,
Feet of clay,

Greedy, crooked politicians,
Businessmen,
Prim, proper women, fishwives,
Who minded other people's manners,

With lack of compassion.
Hollywood improved upon
The novel, made it lush, romantic,
Wiser, kinder,

With the hopefulness that the
Censors would be mollified,
The public titillated,
Yet comforted.

Lana Turner, for once,
Cast fake glamour aside
For moving humanity,
As did the entire, superb cast.

In those days, few predicted
That the floodgates would open
On the crass, sinister,
Serial killers, brutal heroes.

The town we all lived in
Was, like the town we
Actually resided in, a potpourri,
Of good, bad, and often indifferent.

Home for the Holidays, 1954

It was the last Christmas all our family gathered
At my grandparents, my mother's parents' house,
How wonderful, those days were—
And how short!

Like any kid of 10, I looked forward
To my presents, to opening my presents,
As the days, themselves, opened themselves to me,
One by one by one, courtesy of God and nature.

Back home, 60 miles south,
"Young at Heart," in Cinemascope and color,
A musical, co-starring Doris Day and Frank Sinatra,
Was playing at the Delft theater.

What days they were!
Movie previews for "Rear Window,"
"Track of the Cat," "Duel in the Sun,"
The throne-room procession in "The Egyptian."

As soon as we came in sight of the place,
My mother exclaimed, "Oh, look how Dad
Has decorated all the windows with lights!
Don't they look nice?"
                    They shine, now, only in Art.

Blue Xmas

On winter evenings in the early 1950's,
My mother and I would walk to town
For early evening, holiday shopping,

And on our way, would notice
Two large, residential evergreen-trees,
Trimmed in all-blue lights,

And, on an uptown street, also, those nights,
Would notice a small crèche
In a jewelry store window,

Poignant against the night, and
Snow and wind and cold and ice—
And this, its distance in Time's distance.

The Old Masters

What are they worth, really,
Besides millions paid by eccentrics?
They change nothing,

Neither the breath or its motion,
Or the doom of its destination.
Still they exist, they persist,

Far beyond their original impetus,
Subjects, politics, pride, commissions,
All of them a matter of vanity—

In both those who created
And those who sat—yet not quite in vain—
For, lovely in themselves, they remain—
<u>They remain</u>.

Signs

In the early and mid-1950s,
My mother and I would sometimes
Stop in the late afternoons,
On our way home from uptown shopping,

Outside the Delft movie theater,
To peruse posters, stills, and billboards,
Of current and coming attractions, to see
"if anything looked good, was worth seeing."

The theater, the days, the years, now, all are gone,
As are those certain selves we were, and
Seemed to be then—along with the films—
All of them passing gems.

Heaven

It is not,
As so many think,
In the future.

It is not,
As so many think,
In greed, power, lucre.

It is in
Our fragile, mortal, passing lives,
If it is in anything.

Like the black wooden clock,
Which sat atop my grandmother's refrigerator,
Until its time came, its own time came, that is.

It is in
The simple, human things,
Doomed as they are, to oblivion,

As Mother, Dad, and me
Sit together at our kitchen-table,
Eating corn-on-the-cob, in 1953, in summer.

The summer of 1962

I graduated from high school,
In June, at the top of my class,
A member of the National Honor Society,
Co-editor of the annual,

And editor in-chief
Of the school newspaper
Which won state and national
Journalism awards, that year.

I was filled with hope, anyway,
For the future, with my love
Of films and my writing,
But I entered college that fall.

As a secondary ed. English major,
In order to get a deferment
From the draft, which loomed over
Young men, even before Vietnam.

I will never forget that Monday
Morning, early in August,
Mother came upstairs,
To relay the news she had

Just heard on the radio.
"Don't be upset," she said,
"but the news just said
Marilyn Monroe died."

As so many have since,
Along with so many youthful
Hopes, dreams, and ambitions.

Mother and I walked to town
That August, too, under skies
Still, more or less, of blue,

While the earth, the gods,
The fates, themselves, remained silent,
Of all only the years-to-come, knew.

Honore Daumier: The Third Class Carriage

Nothing lasts. Everything changes.
Yet in the paint, she exists,
Continues, persists,
However humble in life, ordinary.

She—the poor, that is—
Never were among the well-off,
Comfortable, lucky.
Nevertheless she remains,

In the paint,
If only in the paint,
In Art's privileged conveyance
Of poignance, durability, and Beauty.

Eros at McDonald's

Today, a young man, early 20s,
Wearing shirt, pants, socks, cap, shoes,
Sits across from me,
In a restaurant,

And as I eye him, I try to imagine him,
Naked, totally naked, cock included
In the whole truth and nothing but,
In his whole truth and nothing but.

Fascists deny, condemn, love and lust between men,
Preferring separation, isolation, warfare, instead,
Yet in spite of that, I have
Already joined with him, in poetry and emotion.

In Memory of Thom Gunn, Gay Poet

I was born in 1944,
And realized by the early grades,
That I was attracted to men.
Handsome movie actors, and

A couple boys in first grade,
Gave the alert.
Bullies yelled epithets,
Like sissy—not gay, then.

Do the straights, by contrast,
Offer such a glowing record—
Thousands of deaths for
Every "major" battle won?

In time,
All lives,
All time, is lost,
All time is at a loss.

When I was young, I wanted
To take the two I loved most—
One in high school; one in college—
In my mouth.

But poetry is a mouth, too,
Even as time departs.
Eros' flame endures
Secure, in Apollo's art.

Travel

We traveled by car and train.
Everywhere we went we saw
Persons, places, things,
Their images plastered in our face.

As far as our eyes could see—
Like intimate strangers,
If only for a moment, the moment,
Each one of them familiar, and each a mystery.

Perfect

Yellow brick, a movie theater,
It stood for decades, until demolished,
After the top of the hill,
In the small town adjoining ours,

The nine muses cavorted in
White scroll work in front,
Announcing the brief home for
Transient viewers and films, alike,

Disney animated features,
Double features on their second-run,
At cheaper prices. All the films
Both came and went.

How lucky all of us were then,
Viewers and characters of Life, itself,
Not only the life on the screen,
But in the seats,

Before and after the movies,
Which provided a Technicolored,
Or black-and-white, escape
From the everyday, the ordinary.

In the poem, if only in the poem,
It is 1954, once, now, always, and again,
As Mother, Dad, and myself, age 10,
Ascend the hill in our green DeSoto,

To see Rosemary Clooney, as in the
Back seat I say, "I can't believe I'm
Actually getting to see this picture,"
Another perfect memory at the Perfect
Theatre.

Adonis

Rock Hudson, in later years, expressed embarrassment
At beefcake, bare-chested, he had done,
Stripped to the waist, as a native American,
In "Taza, Son of Cochise" (1954),

As did Paul Newman, in the same movie year,
In his film debut as Basil,
The bare-legged Greek sculptor,
In "The Silver Chalice."

So it has ever been,
Since the time of the classic, bare-assed Greeks,
When this image of human male excellence—
Buff on the outside, hard on the inside—
Was originally foisted upon us.

Imagine

"Imagine if society changed…"
--a gay newsletter

Imagine
If, instead
Of narrowness, bigotry, prejudice,
Schools taught empathy, tolerance, compassion.

Imagine if people tried to
Complement, instead of best,
Each other, in peace.

Imagine
If, instead,
Of egging bullies on,
Or calmly watching the playground debacle,

Teachers and administrators
Taught acceptance and courtesy.
Fire drill: single file, don't rush, don't push…
Imagine.

A Journey to Toronto, 2007

In all that city,
I saw that day,
The swarms unceasingly busy, at work, at play,
Ant-like in size and duty, yet bound to decay,

Of them all, only one made
A human impression upon me, her face,
A woman weeping in a car's back seat, passing by me,
As a fellow resident of that familiar emotional place.

Music

I remember that on certain human
Afternoons and evenings in the 1950's and 1960's,
My mother would come into our living-room
And say, "I think I'll play the piano,"

And as I sat in a chair,
She would say as she played old songs
Like "The Broadway Melody,"
"Why don't you sing along, sing, too? Join in?"

<u>Who has time for anything like that these days?</u>
The days arrive one by and one, and so depart.
But certain memories remain, and others return
To be played on poetry's harp.

Mood Music

It really got underway in the 1940s's,
As the background scores
For film melodramas and love stories,
Intended as an escape from war.

Today, a blond male, twenty-something,
Bare-assed and beautiful, enters the
Courtyard, at the baths, to sun
Himself, reclines on a chaise-lounge,

Lights a cigarette, self-contained,
Self-possessed, puts a leg up,
And, in so doing,
Moves both my loins and heart.

Graffiti

He loves her.
She loves him.
He loves him.
She loves her.

Initials, epithets, scrawled
On subway walls,
Toilet stalls,
All expressing the nature of Nature.

*

The naked young man sits on the edge of a tub.
The naked young woman reclines inside the tub.

So it has been, has it ever been, since
God split the parts,

Leaving them to seek to combine, to recombine,
In all their needs and wishes.

Little wonder the mechanics, impossibility,
Of the thing, so often results in clenched
Fists, angry words, smashed dishes.

Milk

In honor of Harvey Milk
And Sean Penn's film about him (2008)

If it is love,
What else can matter?
Life is a march from dark to dark.

Colors, races, sexes.
Other men can only kill.
Awaken the human heart.

The Mortal Heaven

I remember that early winter day in 1968,
I was teaching at a university in Wisconsin,

Mother, Dad, and I stopped to shop
At a shopping-mall, which Dad drove us to.

As Mother and I hurried to a gift stores,
Where we found pretty figurines, by fate or chance,

Of an 18th-century lady and gentleman,
In a time, that time,

When time still remained for us, the three of us,
In the life we had then—if only then.

Eros

Two youths meet,
As in classic Greece,

In the modern Midwest,
Combining lives, limbs, tongues, wrists.

*

Where the bee sucks,
There suck I,
Between a naked youth's
Open thighs.

*

Through all the years,
I remember that 1960's street boy, who said,
"Wanna fight?"—wishing only
That it had been, "Wanna fuck?"—instead.

*

It is a warm spring day,
As I notice two college boys playing tennis.
As I walk by, I eye them quietly, privately,
Like the player at chess... I wonder if they guess.

Sheet Music

As soon as my mother graduated
From high school in 1926, her mother
Found her an office job 60 miles south.

From then until his death in 1936,
My mother was the legal secretary
To L.A. Lyon, a local attorney.

In those years, she would, also, stop
To shop at a downtown music-store,
Where she purchased sheet-music.

Waltzes, fox-trots, and songs
From early movie musicals such as
"The Broadway Melody," "Gold Diggers
Of 1933."

From 1936, until she retired in 1942,
She next became the secretary to the
Town realtor-bank president,

His surviving son-in-law, and their
Associate, a Harvard Law School graduate
--prominent local businessmen,

Who hoarded, so that others might
Have less—just as I write these poems,
So that others might have more.

Homophobia—Provinces of

They live all their lives, they think,
In one set, certain, small place,
All the while traveling incessantly
Through vast darknesses of space,

And sing hymns on Sunday,
All week acquire lucre,
And, generation after generation,
Send their leaf, their flower,

To kill or be killed, in war,
Finding fault, really, only
In the sensitive boy or young man
Who lives, at home, with his mother.

Memories of the College Gymnasium, Early 1960s

Tall, dark-blond, hirsute,
He stood naked after his shower,
Drying himself slowly,
In front of all the others,

As an exhibitionist,
A college shower-room star,
Beautiful long-legged prickman,
For nature to embrace, time to mar.

*

Blond, hair close-cropped,
Smooth-limbed, a joy to behold,
A phys.ed. major, an assistant
Swim instructor, red swim-trunked,

Once I seized the chance to see
Him totally naked, cock included,
As he stood by his locker, a
Modern athlete in the classic mould.

Singer—in Memory of Miss Peggy Lee

If I could have been there then,
Known you when, as a young girl, you played
Hopscotch and marbles, jumped rope,
Who am I not to believe in miracles?

If I could have known you then,
Under clouds of white and skies of blue,
Dreaming dreams—some of which came true—
I would have known the first, the original, you.

Before the hotels, lobbies, and limos,
The men you had and who had you,
The songs of what life is all about.
When do they tell you; when do you find out?

Now the years are over, the vagrant days are gone.
Other girls, newcomers, skip rope,
Play hopscotch and marbles,
The big, black cars move on—

And eternity—a mere second—is empty.
Did you think singing over him, his body dead,*
That it is a little like seeing god dead?—
Like a phrase from some tune, old as the moon,

That keeps going through your head—
Life and death both undecipherable, unsurvivable?
Only the vinyl's truly faithful, after
The breath is gone—
The vinyl on which you—the you most you—
Still lives—and will live on.

A note on the above poem: *Peggy Lee sang at the funeral of
Louis Armstrong, in 1971.

Images

Can a life be summed up
By an image or two
--or at the very least—suggested?
Perhaps so…

Consider, for instance, how Norma Jean
Felt, may have felt, when someone she loved,
Whether Aunt Ana Lower, Grace McKee Goddard,
Or Johnny Hyde, died.

But, also consider how Marilyn felt,
May have felt, even in the jungle of death and wrong,
That there is a kind of victory, even so, in the flow,
In every film or song that, somehow, lives on.

Truths

There are various truths.
One is the factual, the actual.
There is also the poetic,
Also actual, but of feeling,
Deeper and more revealing.

Life is all and what we have,
However much under the jungle's curse.
We will never really know
The meaning of water, of life, that is—
Until that day we die of thirst.

Domestic

Odd the things, the moments,
One remembers
In preference to all
Those one forgets
Or holds in abeyance

Trivial in the overall
Scheme of things, perhaps,
But, at least at the time,
In their time,
Literally momentous.

The way Mother was there,
Always there, afternoons
When I came home from school,
My heart aching or breaking
Over adolescent minutiae or ambition.

She might be watching
A soap opera on television,
Or ordering a case of Kist pop, for me,
With its alluring favors:
Orange, red, cream soda

Or in the backyard
Taking down clothes from the line,
Which she hung out, she said, for the
Smell of freshness—like us, like everything,
Dependent on the ozone.

In memory of C.P. Cavafy

In reading him, one realizes
The brevity of erotic encounters,
But, equally, of all human relationships,
Even the ones lasting lifetimes, decades.

In reading him, one, also, realizes
The sense and yet senselessness of things,
Of loves experienced and lost, every bit
As lost those that never were,
Or merely imagined.

For years, decades, he moved quietly,
Little noticed, between home and work,
A modest bespectacled clerk,
Conversant with both gods and mortals,
Yet considered commonplace, ordinary.

Holbein the Younger: The Madonna Of Burgomaster Meyer

It is difficult to believe, now,
How this possessed,
However left unsatisfied,
The human imagination for more than
A thousand years.

The Madonna, tall as an oak,
Holds the Infant God, too small,
In the palm of her hands,
While several others stand about
As bystanders:

Joseph, to the right, a mere man,
And John the Baptist, the less favored cousin,
To the left, and to the right,
A stern little nun, image of many
Authoritarians to come.

FDR

A traitor to his class,
Some said,
But not to the human race,
As many in power have been.

The wealthy, powerful,
Supposedly above
The common run, "better,"
Better off, but often inhuman.

A victim of polio,
He himself
May have learned
From adversity, a degree of compassion.

At any rate, that
Human greatness is not
In lording over, or driving under,
But in a helping hand; a lifting up.

Dante

I do not congratulate him, or anyone,
For siding with power,
For viewing human agony, misery,

With insouciance, from a distance,
Nor do I see glory
Of a favored few, instead of universal mercy.

Better fit that the humble human
Have its hour, if only its hour,
A mere brief existence, which is all
Reality is, anyway.

In fact, I think that randy young Italian,
Playing his own piccolo
Into his sex object,

Whether male or female,
Both in the short run and long run,
Had more truck with nature's actual,
On-going contagion.

The Jester—Bob Hope (1903—2003)

Into each life, it's been said,
Some rain must fall.
But in some lives, more rain,
In others, less rain.

Each life must end,
In time, sometime, within Time.
But in some lives, more time.
In other lives, less time.

I think, now, of all the anonymous
Young men, glimpsed in his audiences,
Headed for nothing much but oblivion,
Just as he returned to sound-stages,
Estates, special Oscars.

Still, in the end, only death
Has the last laugh,
Bringing an end, a mere end,
To everyone and everything.

The Darling

Seeming heiress of all the ages,
Blond, catered to, wearing the latest fashions,
Her life a part of Life, if only her part

A goddess alive, but only momentarily,
Riding the stage like an immortal,
Until the arrow pierced her heart.

Eros

To C.S. and C.W.B.

It was sex, of course,
But not merely that.
Or it was that, but also the desire
For friendship, affection.

Most men not only
Have sex with women,
But callously compete,
And sometimes murder, other men.

I used to laugh
At the segregation of the sexes
In gym and lockers and showers
After gym.

As if only opposites attracted,
As if only heterosexuality existed,
As I caught, thanks to the system,
Many eyefuls within my vision.

A Pole Dancer—Toronto, 2004, Remington's

A young man tonight,
Tall, brunette, handsome,
And completely naked,
Bumps and grinds

With real rhythm, panache,
At a strip bar in Toronto,
In a time of an
Unjust war,

Typical yet divine,
The epitome of erotic perfection,
To me, and to fascists,
Also, the symbol of male beauty, eros,

Which—not war, not poverty,
Injustice, cruelty, death—
They view, would view, as sin,
Perhaps as the ultimate abomination.

Dido—Queen of Carthage; Lover of Aeneas

It is not the knowledge
That things do not last,
In fact, cannot last,
That bothers one. One accepts that.

Of course, to perish oneself
Is quite another thing
From standing back,
Surveying time's passage and final result—
On others—

Whether with empathy and compassion
--or, as with most men—
Without them—
Lacking humanity for the human.

This even was not the worst,
Death's curse.
The worst was to witness
His turned back; the city in flames.

In Memory of Susan Hayward

We are at the positive place
At the moment of our birth
And, at our death, the negative one.

A feisty redhead from Brooklyn,
Spotted as NYC clerk
By the wife of David Selznick.,

She was whisked to Hollywood,
Screen tested as Scarlett O'Hara,
Lost the part, but gained admittance

To the studio system, where she
Climbed, determined to get
To the top, one rung at a time,

Making a career, indelible impressions,
As heroines and vixens alike,
Amid an Oscar and five nominations,

Only, in the end, to be at
Exactly the worst place, on-location,
For a picture in the southwest desert,

Near the scene of atomic tests,
Developing a brain tumor, and dead at 57,
Her films, the enduring medium.

Praise

Praise… there's no need to praise
Politics, munitions, religions,
The poor, suffering world is controlled
By them.

Praise… well, the dead past is dead,
Beyond redemption,
The days, alone, enable us to live
And perish.

Praise, anyway, the bygone days,
The loved ones we knew,
The days we spent with them,
The days that contained, portrayed,
But could not keep them.

Praise does no good, of course,
It does not repeal oblivion.
Nothing's so denied, vulnerable, as the
Human.

Praise, anyway, the father who painted,
Who put a roof over our head,
The mother who kept house, comforted,
And was human.

The Hollywood Outside of Hollywood

Anonymous, nondescript men and women,
In the photograph, line up,
In a city, outside a 1940's theater,
Waiting to pay admission, to get in,

Outside, for the time being,
Modestly dressed, marginal,
Used or ignored by powers-that-be,
Except to be expended, taken-for-granted.

Yet citizens who escaped if only
For a couple hours, at the movies,
Each time, now and then, again and again,
In a darkened cave, a comfort zone,

Where life on the screen seemed
What it should be, or was then,
If only then: a newsreel, previews,
Cartoon included.

I should know...
How often,
So often,
I was one of them.

Autumn Song

Nothing lasts.
Everything expires in its life,
In the very motion,
Heaven and hell together,
With a common destination of extinction.

Once it was life, and only life,
And love, ample, new,
The years and people
Filled the cupboard, our life's cupboard.
The leaves, as usual,

At nature's cue, turn, lose, color.
The young arrivestes both see, and do not see, this.
The solipsists of all generations, ages.
Yet everything perishes,
Even in the comfortable, aloof suburbs.

The Train, 1930's

The train moves
Across the landscape,

Indenting it,
Without indenting it,

Both by dark of night
And light of the sun.

The hoboes and young men,
Homeless, envy the townsfolk,

Comfortable, safe in their beds,
While the townsfolk,

Hearing the locomotives,
Dream only of escape, of freedom,

In all cases, of some other road, path taken,
That, somehow, might lead to a different destination.

Cinema Verite

Perhaps it was Doris Day who
Glittered in buckskin in
"Calamity Jane."
Marilyn certainly did,
In "Gentlemen Prefer Blondes,"
"There's no Business Like
Show Business."

It also was Ethel Merman
In "Call Me Madam," as the
"hostess with the mostest,"
Sally Adams.
We can't revisit the actual,
Inactual past, in the same
Ways, we can visit them.

Memory's a fragile palace,
Gaudy and haunted,
And partial at best,
No substitute for what and all
We loved and knew.
But we made do
With what we have,
As best we can.

I sometimes like to picture, in the 20's,
My mother, who was then
Miss Lillian Mager—
English, pronounced may-ger,
Hard "g"—sitting at piano,

Or, in the 1930's, my parents
Before they were married,
Walking to and going in
To see a double feature,
Up the hill, at the Perfect.

Mother used to refer, not to
Pictures so often, but
Actors' names, in a moment
Of recognition—
Leon Janney, Lyle Talbot,
She'd say, of players,
All a part of life's
Brief, all too brief,
Vanishing parade.

An Invitation to the Voyage

The ship has many rooms and floors.
It existed long before any of its
Current passengers.
None have met or seen its owner,
Although some have pretended to.

In any case, the owner is only
Present in its absence,
Either that or its absence is its
Presence; its absent-presence,
Its essence.

In any case, there are divisions,
According to age, heritage, lucre,
Circumstance.
Billions of passengers have
Come and gone, then were discarded.

This does not seem to worry or
Annoy unduly
The current lot, who spend their time
In more or less animal appetites and
Ambitions.
Only the fact each ticket has a
Limit is certain.

Durer: Rabbit

It looks out
Seeing nothing
With seeming sight,
A conundrum,

For ages,
Over the ages.
Dumb lifelike
But not alive

Except as images,
As paint,
Unaware of itself,
Existence, endurance,

Its image sufficient
In and to itself,
And for us, its witnesses,
Likewise beings of nature,
But with comprehension.

Prophecy

My mother's brother met
A girl in Texas at a Methodist
Social, before he was shipped
Overseas to China, in 1942.

He married her in 1946,
And they lived in Michigan
For ten years, before
They moved to Texas.

Sometimes, my uncle would
Ask my mother to let me
Travel by train to visit them.
I really didn't' want to.

"You know, he might as well
Learn. He'll have to go
To the military," he said.
My mother's brother-in-law,

Her sister's husband, said,
As a career Air Forceman,
"You have feminine ways.
The service would do you good."

No doubt, shed my hair.
No doubt, end my sensitivity.
I knew as soon as I heard the
1960 presidential debates,

"Quemoy and Matsu," that
The coming years would see
A hot war, somewhere.
The compass pointed to Vietnam,

Or the military-industrial
Complex did. It did a lot of those
People, both domestic and foreign,
Nothing but harm.

I studied, went to college,
And taught there while jobs lasted.
The years kill everyone we love.
No need to rush things.

Our doom forecast, foreknown,
And certain.

Five and Dime

In our town, it was
J. J. Newberry's,
Gilt lettering above
The glass doors,
With brown wooden trim.

Wooden floors inside,
A bookkeeper who wore
Her visor in back of the
Premises, up in an office.

Displays of knick knacks,
Bric-a-brac, jewelry,
Cosmetics, books
Remaindered, at cheaper prices.

Crèche pieces, at xmas,
Records anytime, flowers,
Hours that came and went,
All of them passing fancies.

One summer day, in 1966,
The record played "Cabaret,"
I bought a blue parakeet
I brought home, I named "Baby."

My father painted the store
In the 1950's. It's closed, now,
Long since; in later years
Became a Ben Franklin.

How happy were the days,
Their idle pleasures,
Problems, taking our loves,
Comic books, movie magazines,

In the end, as if debris,
In a flood,
An unseen flood of time,
Of years, in silent succession.

An Xmas Memory, 1952

In memory I stand, age eight,
Near the second floor balcony,
Of the downtown J.C. Penney's
Store ladies section,

As usual, taking it all in,
Not with any plan for a
Poem many decades ahead,
But present and accounted-for,

As I eye the customers
On the first floor,
As well as the cars passing by
On the street outside.

Mother, whom I often accompany
On shopping forays, is
Looking for a good,
Sensibly priced winter coat,

Which, it turns out, she finds
In a red woolen cloth,
With large fake fur gray collar.
I tell her I wish it was real fur.

Like rich women have.
My mother, all the same, beams
In the seasonal store gleam,
As does the plump female clerk,

Happy, expectant, at the
Thought of her commission.
So many things seemed real, then,
That are now present only in my cranium.

The MGM Musicals

They were among the first films
I ever saw, taken by my mother,
"The Unfinished Dance,"
"Easter Parade," "Summer Stock,"
"3 Little Words," "Royal Wedding."

They were not alive, exactly,
Although they were living,
And although not really real,
They had a certain kind of reality,

All glamour, all beauty, all talent,
As well as all singing and dancing.
And they were real to us, if only
For the brief hours we saw them.

I remember coming home, early 1954,
After seeing a matinee preview
For "Kiss Me Kate," which ended
With the statement:

"The greatest of all great
MGM musicals." "I just have to see it,"
I said, after telling my mother
What the preview said.

My mother replied, "Oh, they say
That about them all."
Nevertheless, we went, caught up
In the spell of characters and songs
Which, inside, have never ended.

Edgar

To begin with, it was the name
My grandmother, mother's mother,
Wanted me to have, because
It was the name of my uncle,

My grandmother's only son,
Who, at the time, 1944,
Was serving behind a desk in
China with the "Flying Tigers."

My mother, all the same, insisted
That my first name be Leon,
After my father, whose own
Middle name was Earl.

Everything went well enough
Until, in 1949, I entered
Kindergarten, a nice little boy,
Loved at home,

Taken to grade school, like
A lamb to the slaughter.
The hags of the town instructed
Their children and grandchildren

To use it as a weapon of derision,
Yelling it from busses, cars,
On streetcorners, on my walks
To and from school, the movies,

And always on the cursed playground.
The writer allegedly named
Shakespeare wrote,
"What's in a name?...

"A rose by any other
Name, would smell
As sweet."...
He was mistaken.

On Moonlight Bay (1951)

Once upon a time, in its prime,
Hollywood stood for
Glamour and sentiment,
For escape from the ordinary.

Warner Bros., early fifties,
Offered the rhyming team
Of "Doris Day and Gordon MacRae,"
A teens and twenties small town,

A mischievous younger brother,
Played by Billy Gray;
Parents by Leon Ames and Rosemary
De Camp; their maid by Mary Wickes.

The critics were the worse,
Taking the movies to task
For studio-bound sets,
Superb art direction,

Because they were escapist,
Human stories,
The very things that made them
Special, out of the ordinary.

I used to think of death,
For all of that,
At times, watching them,
A rumor that, one day,

Something or other
Would spoil things,
In spite of everything,
Bring things to an end,

In a reality all too real
Or unreal. Still, what a
Pleasure it was to witness
A make-believe world, then,

Which brought out the best,
Not the coarse, crude, or common.
Where all kinds of talent proved,'
In many ways to be fantastic.

House of Wax (1953)

The big, original hit in 3-D
Came to our small town
Delft theatre in a
Sweltering July.

I wanted to see it,
And was repaid for my
Curiosity with
Nightmares all summer.

Vincent Price played
The horribly scarred villain.
A fire victim, who turned
Killer, to people his new museum.

He chased Phyliss Kirk,
The heroine, on 19th century
New York streets, bluish-hued,
Actually studio sets,

As Mother and I sat
In our seats preoccupied
With the clumsy paper glasses,
With plastic green lenses,

Worn so we could see
A ping-pong ball, for instance,
Come at us in the audience,
Or seen to.

When the show was over,
We walked home past an
Ice-cream parlor, neighbors
In a car, who asked,

"What was it like?"
"It was horrible" my mother
Answered, although we were able
To return home to our mortal haven.

Domestic II

One day you'll come full circle.
You'll remember, revere,
The perishing years,
The good people,

Even as you did
In their time,
At the time,
Of the years you shared with them.

The world judges on Mammon,
And how the square peg fits,
But the artist sees the bits
Nature offers, its flowers, when

At times the jungle relents
In its cruelty, tribulation.
"We tried to make things
Nice for you," my mother said.

Others talk of gods so cruel
The punishment is eternal,
As, in a way, its way,
Death, of course, is.

I talk of gods, precious,
Because merely human,
Merely mortal,
For the kindness there was, and is.

One day, you'll come full circle.
You'll miss their day to day presence.
The people you love, and loved,
For their purely human essence.

Ways That Are Dark—In Memory of Val Lewton

Erudite, overweight,
He grasped what fate
Had cast him:

Making something
Unusual, subtle,
Of low-budget horror pictures,

And allowed to do so,
Because they not only
Filled the bill,

But turned a profit.
Horror is everyday,
He seemed to convey,

In the mean-spirited
Diabolists; in the
Body snatchers,

In the time and tide of
History, cruel men
As animal as any leopard.

The shadows were atmospheric,
And powerful in their suggestion.
The world, after all,

Is, indeed, a charnel-house,
No need to pretend,
Or to pretend with silly
Monster costumes.

Val Lewton wrote and produced notable RKO films in the 1940's, including "The Cat People," "The Leopard Man," "The Seventh Victim," and "The Body Snatchers," all alluded to in the poem above.

Spring Song

The flowers come to life
As the rains once more descend

As Persephone, Pluto's wife,
Rises from the earth again.

The Godfather Trilogy

(1972, 1974, 1989)

Gangsters came with prohibition,
Invaded the screen,
But crime didn't really
Begin to pay

Off and on screen,
Until it went, supposedly,
Respectable, in the guise
Of family, commerce, religion,

With a dash of patriotism
Thrown in, all excuses
For the means to the
Domestic, capitalist end,

Whether a rain of bullets,
A horse's head in a bed,
Whatever it took,
Brando's jowls padded,

Pacino aging, his face
Rounder, more corrupt,
All the way to fratricide,
The Vatican.

It even had Rota's lush
Theme music, soap opera
Upgraded from luckless,
Unwed tramps and mothers,

To the big time,
Where crime paid,
Millions in the coffers,
As well as a mantel of Oscars.

The Last Picture Show (1971)

Movies and movie magazines
Came to the villages, towns,
As well as the cities,
Temples to illusion,

As if life were not an illusion,
Dotting many a landscape,
With magazines briefly housed
On many a dime-store-type shelf,

All as an escape hatch
From monotony, boredom,
Bullies, the wind that
Blew everything away,

Even when no one
Noticed it, oldsters,
And youngsters, in war,
Each day dropping one by one.

Even the previews had promise,
An exciting canvas up on the screen,
Not strict like church or school,
But an alternative to rules,

Judgments, caste systems,
Sexual, socio-economic,
Where once a week,
Or as often as one could,

At the weekend matinee,
Or weeknight school night,
Home right after 9 p.m.,
Viewers and Illusion became as One.

The Hypochondriac Gossip Mailman

To him,
The only good news,
Was always bad news.

Savonarola

Let's face it,
The gods, many, three, or one,
Are made in men's images
Of what their gods are.

Before the Greeks,
The barbarians envisioned
Animals as gods,
Rather than the Human.

It seems it depends
On whose vision of god it is.
At one time, naked males,
Athletes, were seen

As being ideal
As well as merely human.
He, at any rate, used
His views to boil people in oil.

It's like the airplane.
It depends on the usage.
But men would kill without them.
They always did.

So he ranted and railed,
During his moment,
As do they all, despoiling
Life in the process.

By Them Who Dwell in Darkness

One said.
They said.
It was written.

The reply
Unheard, unheeded.
The only sin is cruelty.
There are all kinds of darkness.

Beyond the Forest (1949)

Proust, traveling by train,
Observed disdainfully
The cramped, ugly villages,
Pockets of ignorance,

Until he considered that
One, or some, of them,
Might house, might imprison,
A Madame Bovary.

The film Bette Davis and critics
Deplored, captured her essence
As a vixen, the venom of the
Female, trapped by circumstances.

Those that praise small towns
Often did so from the vantage
Point of Hollywood, popularity,
Patting the Yahoos on the back,

For mindless conformity,
Thoughtless acceptance,
Adherence to the big boys' rules,
Man on top, woman subservient,

Just as millionaire composers
Rhapsodized the joys of
Poverty, those things,
During the depression.

Rosa Moline, nonetheless,
Had spit,
Tired of the blast furnaces
That blocked her view,

Tired of the doctor husband,
Who took preserves for payment,]
A virago, a vixen,
Both using and used by

A rich Chicago businessman,
For his amusement,
During his fishing trips,
To the provinces.

Listen, small towns trapped
People besides Madame Bovary.
They trapped Prousts, too,
And mocked their idealism.

Ironically, Rosa's foray
To Chicago seemed
Film noirish, too,
The timeless lot of any outsider.

"A town like this is hard
On a woman like Rosa,"
A character says in the film,
As life is hard on everyone,

Every step of the way,
And ultimately at the end.
Dead on the tracks, more than
The train to Chicago abandoned.

Mildred Pierce (1945)

The ads read, "The kind of
Woman most men want,
But shouldn't have,"
The typical come-on.

Mildred, soft-spoken,
Tremulous, swathed in furs,
Joan Crawford, in her comeback,
By the ocean,

Ready to give up, to jump,
Tired of being the patsy,
The fall guy, the good,
Long-suffering woman.

Short-changed by everyone:
An adulterous husband,
An ungrateful daughter,
A crooked business partner.

Cheated by nature, too,
Her neglected younger daughter
Succumbing to pneumonia
The one weekend Mother was away.

Of course, it was a story.
Few career women were
So lucky, so fast, creating a
Chain of prosperous restaurants

By starting with pies and cakes
In her suburban kitchen.
Everything, anyway,
In the inflection,

Crawford under-acting
All the way to the Oscar,
Done in herself, decades later,
By the adopted daughter

She had left out of her will.
For a while only, the ether exits,
The false hopes everyone brings
To life, the transient place in the sun.

Tea and Sympathy (1956)

The plight of the sissy,
The "sister boy" in its terminology,
It, at least, as play and movie,
Hit the nail a bit on the head.

All those crewcut boys,
Athletes, draft-bait,
Gung-ho for the military,
Bred on John Wayne movies.

No wonder the headmaster's wife
Tired of it. Hollywood censored
The real deal: the nude beach,
In the play, with teacher and student.

Still, it portrayed the ostracism,
Cold shoulder, the baiting,
Alternating, toward the hatred
Of sensitivity, insight, emotion.

I never regretted, regardless,
My sensibility, my love
Of the arts, of the human,
Or for several young men.

The sissy-boy, good student,
Who walked home alone, lived within,
Seeing generation after generation
Go down in war, to seed, to greed.

The Legend of John Wayne

Born Marion Morrison, Midwest,
Well, he couldn't help that.
A California football player,
Then bit player,

Discovered by director
John Ford, who, it was said'
Was the only man Wayne
Allowed to talk down to him.

In any case, he rode the range,
Engaged in one celluloid battle
After another, and the kids
Followed him in life, in death,

As in "Sands of Iwo Jima,"
Filmed on the backlot.
His only actual service
Was on film, in make-believe.

But the world swallowed it.
First, it was the Indians,
Then the Nazis, then the commies.

It was always something, someone,
Race or nation or other.
There were some good films, too,
With relative realism: "True Grit."

"Stagecoach," "Red River,"
"The Quiet Man," "The Searchers."
Off-screen, Red-baiting,
Witch-hunts for liberal

And fellow-traveler alike;
The several wives and children.
When the actual end came, was it
Glorious or just a big nothing?

The Greatest Show on Earth (1952)

The movies were the show
Within the show of life.
Each beckoned,
Whether seen or missed.

It's 1952 on the calendar,
Dad in the driver's seat,
Mother in front, me in back,
Give a lift to a neighbor-girl,

From up the next street,
An honor student and nurse-to-be,
Who mentions she's seen it,
The DeMille circus movie,

And "it's good." Recommendation
Enough for movie-addict me,
As I campaign to see it,
And we attend,

To see the animals,
The aerialists,
The center rings and parade,
The train wreck,

Myself at age eight,
Innocent, present-minded,
Not yet able to see time,
The years ahead, or behind,

As the real, ultimate,
Unavoidable Train Wreck.
Both home and films were
The happy shows still playing

At the time, then,
If only for the time, then,
Mother, Dad, and me, we three,
The even greater show.

Cabaret (1972)

Too bad life isn't a musical,
The theatre with its
Petty egos, ups and downs,
With a happy ending.
Well, life isn't like that.

The bigots play for keeps.
Take Berlin, early 1930s,
The British writer, in the film,
A bisexual, meaning really gay,
And Sally Bowles, English, too,

In Isherwood's stories,
But Americanized for the
Zippy, zesty film version,
With choreography by Bob Fosse,
Screenplay by Jay Presson Allen.

You have to admit it, though:
Some people have talent,
But this time with a difference
And a vengeance: no one was
Fooled by the fools' play,

Sure the smoke-filled joint
Was heady, amoral, brazen,
But the reality outside was worse:
Manly, apple-cheeked, blond, Aryan,
We've all met them on the playground,

And when facism herds them,
Well, the child's ball bounced
Down the stairs, the steps,
At the end of the film, didn't it?
So much for the state of the world.

Gone to the commoners,
The unfeeling conformists,
Militarists, eros-haters.
The minorities condemned.
The earth, itself, in lethal disarray.

White Christmas (1954)

Released nationally in late 1954,
It played the Delft Theatre
In February 1955, over a
Three-day weekend.

At the Saturday matinee, I sat
With my neighbor friend,
Watching the screen come alive
With World War II camaraderie, fun,

With the promise of
Heterosexual couplings,
Happy ever after endings,
A general who seemed like Eisenhower,

The wonderful music of Irving Berlin:
"Sisters," "Count Your Blessings,"
"The Best Things Happen While
You're Dancing." They often did.

I loved them all, and this one
So much I told my mother, "You've
Got to see it, too," and so,
With Mother, Monday night,

We went. I went again.
My neighbor friend moved to Texas
In 1958, Vietnam in the 1960's,
And died, age 40, of cancer.

The best things, the good things,
In those years, often happened
On the screen, and sometimes
In life, too,

But the days came and went,
Because of the way
The world was, the way it is,
All of us, its passing illusions.

The House by the River (1939-)

Mother and Dad lived in our house
Five years before I was born.
For three years before that,
They had rented.

Mother used her secretarial wages
Wisely, saving for a rug here,
A mirror there, and windfalls
When Dad got good painting jobs.

Beloved, if I relayed all
The ups and downs, traumas,
Of the years, it would sound
Like a rant, like the days

After the last mine left,
A federal judge in 1979,
Let the company stop its pumps,
Which now allowed seepage

To low-lying regions,
Our house, built about 1927,
Had only one previous owner,
A jeweler, was built with a

Solid stone foundation,
That my parents, also, were,
An edifice surviving onslaughts
Of weather, the years none survive,
The years which themselves perish,

Decades of bullies, recessions,
The draft, wars and their rumors,
College faculty cutbacks,
A mean, intolerant little town,

My irate uncle, my mother's brother,
Who, retired from the IRS, in 1971,
Angered by my disapproval of
The Vietnam War and Nixon, said,

"We'll write to your employers
Or prospective employers, to see
You never work again."
Culture, it's been said,

Is not the main fray, but what's
Created by the side of the river,
The human life which my parents
And I shared, in spite of everything.

Forever Amber (1947)

During Hollywood's golden age,
It had nearly 60 million
Weekly customers,
And numerous detractors,

Who said it was imagined,
An escape from reality,
Rather than a dull record of it,
Stories about people,

A human canvas, which,
In this case, presented
The best-seller about a
Restoration wench,

Her struggles, courage,
In spite of fickle male lovers
And a variety of circumstances.
In a time of depression and war,

The Legion of Decency got in a
Dither about how many lovers
She would be seen to have,
How she'd be made to suffer,

Indifferent to talent,
Costumes, music, period decor,
The lovely Linda Darnell, in a
Blond wig, as a memorable heroine.

The censors not concerned with
Human empathy, truth, or compassion,
Which the studio,
20th Century-Fox, itself,

Fearful of a backlash,
Acquiesced at least partly to,
Not wishing to be shunned, itself,
At the Almighty Box Office.

Life with Mother

She was my lifetime best friend.
After my father, a victim of
High blood pressure, died
Suddenly in May, 1970,

I returned home. Every step
Of the way we helped each other.
When she had more, she helped me.
When I had more, I helped her.

Everywhere I turned, doors of
Opportunity were closed,
Both near, and far, in those
Years of war and reaction.

Through it all, we maintained
And valued home and hearth.
Only my aunt Elaine, my mother's sister,
Helped us at all, of them all.

I see Mother, driving our car,
A series of them, twice a day
To restaurants for coffee-breaks,
As I called them, patiently listening

To my hopes for a career, also,
Once in the morning to the
Post office box, which finally
Yielded acceptances, publications.

Mother valued life and loyalty.
"I'm a lucky lucky woman," she'd say.
Still a patient friend, at age
Ninety, when, one Sunday afternoon,

She slipped away for good,
After nearly two years at home
In a wheelchair, after she broke her hip.
A real angel, a mortal one, whose
Realm was Earth.

Vera Cruz (1954)

It came to me by accident,
As a Saturday matinee in 1956,
As some of the good things
In life, as well as bad, seem to.

Life can change in a moment.
No morning knows what the
Afternoon may bring,
Or the evening.

I was only 12 when
It came, when it played,
Old for my age,
Precocious, in some ways,
And in other ways innocent,

Aware of art as an alternative,
A world glorious in itself,
A view beyond small minds
And a small town,

A larger canvas,
Available in a seat
For twenty-five cents. Like life,
Pedestrian and yet miraculous.

The adventurers, mercenaries,
Came, were hired to take
A shipment of gold,
To the Mexican port,

Everyone after it:
Highwaymen, diplomats,
A conniving, glamorous countess,
And a horde of peasants.

Lancaster, Cooper,
Darcel, Montiel,
An adventure whose memory,
The memory of Art,

Still lives, will live,
Can live beyond the
Time it was made,
The people who made it,

And the worldly,
Yet innocent,
Sophisticated yet
Believing child who saw it.

Eros in Hollywood

The Puritans were right:
Art's always been an escape hatch,
More on the side of life than death,
Sex than annihilation,
With, of course, exceptions.

To be a movie star, in those days,
Was to be human, and yet also
Supra-human, in terms of
Talent, fame, money,
And sexual glow and opportunity.

The fascists wanted people
To be poor, orderly, narrow,
In a tight fit and content with it.
Still, the screen presented
Life as it should have been,

Household names, happy endings
For all but the villains,
Heroes and heroines
Who survived and overcame obstacles.

And they came, the talented,
For the chance one in a million,
But a chance to achieve
And live in mortal radiance.

So many, if not all, were gay.
Valentino, Novarro, Power, Webb,
Hunter, Hudson, Dietrich, Garbo,
Clift, Hepburn, or bi, like Flynn.

The difference they made was
Fleeting, perhaps, like life's.
All shone at night; some shown
For Many Nights… but all Shone.

As Time Goes By,
The Music of the Years Gone By

It was Gide who said,
His many tears
Had nourished
His books, his philosophy.

Oh beloved you'll never know
The more human world
I wanted for my own family,
And the human family,

The world, unless you
Read these lines, my lines,
How I'd go daily to my
Typewriter, for decades,

As Mother would go to a
Notebook occasionally,
To jot down the simple joys
And routine of life,

A home, a hearth,
In the world,
A part of the world,
Yet apart from the world.

Time may prove both
Breath and life to be a lie,
But those times and
Lives we shared, happened,

A truth, our truth,
My truth—in the now,
The many now's, which have
Now, by now, become—then.

Reflections

These days, these years,
The only way I can visit
Those I loved are
In memory, in reverie,

Or by placing flowers
On graves,
Trimming weeds,
In a kind of protection.

Men say they are somewhere,
The deceased billions,
Howling in pain, or
Floating as emanations.

Neither seems satisfactory,
Nor does the defunct actuality.
Our time together was brief,
The years appearing, disappearing.

Some claim the rings
Exists for the Tree.
To me, the Tree,
Exists for the rings
However momentarily.

I know of one who tells me
She goes walking, goes walking,
In a local cemetery,
Sensing only silence, peace.

Here all is resolved.
The ball one thought lost,
So long ago, and forgot, is found,
At last, at long last, after all.

Sometimes, now, towards
Evening, my own evening,
I recall the times we had,
The people I knew and loved,
Before the final Shadows fall.

Commerce

I remember going to a psychic
Near West Ed Avenue in 2001,
Who said, "You have recently lost
Someone you loved very much."

"When you were young," she said,
"people were jealous of you.
Later you loved a couple young men,
But they didn't love you."

"Everywhere you travel,
A cloud travels with you.
You have a shattered aura.
I'll need money to fix it."

A few years earlier, a male seer,
Through the mails, perhaps,
Came a bit closer to the crux,
At least in my estimation.

"What makes you so fascinating,"
He wrote, "are your contradictions
And complexity. Yet if I had to
Choose one, and only one,

Characteristic for you, it would
Have to be your sensitivity…
It grieves me to realize
The price you paid for it."

Losses

My grandfather, John Mager,
Had a prostate operation in 1945.
His doctor to heal it
"gave him a dose of radium."
He suffered for the next ten years,
Dying of cancer, in 1955.

My grandmother, Jessie Lobb Mager,
Lived on, her last several years
In a Texas nursing home,
For the next fifteen years.
Memory lasts so much longer
Than so-called reality.

Reality, that is, is only one
Among several realities.
The house was closed in 1960,
Sold in 1964. Memory and
Poetry are the only two
Ways I still can visit,

And re-visit, it. Its ten rooms,
Two floors, attic, pantry,
Garage, garden, trees,
Wooden shed filled with magazines,
For the time being, that time
Being while we all, they all, lived.

I, remember how, as a child,
I'd sit by the shed watching
The small patches of lettuce
And beans grow, the morning
Glories nearby, attached to a post.
The glory of all those lost
Mornings, afternoons, and evenings.

Gone with the Wind (1939)

What if the years disappear
With the people?
They do, you know.
Even eternity, or nature,
Cannot repeat, restore, them.

In spite of love, humanity.
It makes no difference.
The world is brutal, a jungle,
Giving, taking, unforgiving,
The wars overcome, ongoing,

Always new and newer ones.
What to make of it?
For a while and a while only,
There is a home, our home,
Our loved ones, our luck,

In having good homes,
Good families, however
Much doomed in time, by Time,
The seconds themselves succumb
In themselves,

Every one of them,
One after one after everyone.
Art's only a kind of substitute.
How short those days were,
How tenuous, and how precious.

In Memory of Veronica Lake

Plain Constance Ockleman
Somehow gained entrée vous
To Paramount, to become
Veronica Lake, the

Passive, impassive blond babe,
Understated for Sturges,
A mannequin, a dream figure,
Opposite Ladd, her male complement.

The peek-a-boo doo, a
Sensation among women and men,
Till its imitation endangered
Women with machinery, weapons.

The magic, or whatever it was,
Lasted only a few years.
A dozen for her of soirees,
Fame and fortune,

For the world, an inferno,
The hapless sent on missions,
Experimented on in death camps.
Where was the love, the mercy?

Our boys fought for another day,
A more decent world,
Which for greed and power,
Other men are ready to betray

Themselves and each other.
Anonymity, rejection, followed,
And finally the exit, death.
What is this crazy world

About, all about, a fan wrote.
She was a movie star who ended
Up with nothing. Briefly
Privileged, the universal end.

In Memory of Grace Kelly

"I'm just a girl from the country,"
As Georgie Elgin, Frank's
Long-suffering, patient wife,
She said in "The Country Girl."

In reality, she was a girl
From Philadelphia, not really
The Main Line, but prosperous,
The daughter of a bricklayer,

With a charm, self-reliance,
Good manners, good looks,
A style like many others,
Yet all her own.

The rule illustrated by the
Exception: lucky on the stage,
In early live television,
Beginning as a model,
Door after door opened,

And when she went Hollywood,
She was ready: fire and ice,
At the same time, a lady,
Yet one with suppressed passion.

Fate seems the key,
Whatever fate is,
On-location in the Mediterranean,
She met her semi-handsome prince,

And for the price of her
Retirement and procreation,
She was given a minor kingdom.
Rumors of discontent,

As the years went, and her fear
That she had been so lucky,
Too lucky. All are losers in the end.
Cinema her lasting station.

Middle School

Seventh and eighth grades
In my time, that time,
1956—1958, were called
junior high.

The best thing about
Them was they ended
The alternate torment and
Isolation of recess.

Home was the still the primary
Comfort zone, haven,
Not church, and not school,
Although I got straight A's,

Although the daughters of
Rich mining officials
Were favored, as they were
To be in years ahead.

At home, several studios
Sold their old films,
Pre-1948, called backlogs,
To television,

Plus series like "Zorro,"
"Stories of the Century,"
"Frontier Doctor,"
"Alfred Hitchcock presents."

Sunday evenings, after church,
I'd peruse myself naked
In my bedroom mirror,
Brunette, thin, with pubic hair.

The future, however mundane,
Remained a mystery ahead.
It was in heaven then, in a way,
But one I knew Time would not
Allow me to keep.

The Author and His Book:

L.E. Ward was born July 5, 1944, as Leon Edgar Ward. "Pennies from Heaven" is his seventh published book of poems, and ninth collection of poetry, containing over 100 poems, written since 2003. His books reflect his lifetime interests: Immersion in the past, both personal and cultural; a criticism of war, intolerance, and materialism; a love of the arts, eros, and human times and relationships, including family, friends, and lovers. "Pennies from Heaven," like its predecessors, looks askance at violence, greed, and fanaticism, yet also concerns itself with beauty, art, and humanism.

Ward, a former university teacher of literature, has also had a prolific prose writing career as an essayist and contributing editor to national film periodical, among others. His writing has received many honors, awards, and award nominations. His books are dedicated to the memory of his beloved parents, Leon Earl Ward (1898-1970) and Lillian Estelle Mager Ward (1908-1999).